ANY GOD WILL DO

Books by Virginia Konchan

The End of Spectacle
Anatomical Gift
Empire of Dirt

ANY GOD WILL DO

Virginia Konchan

Carnegie Mellon University Press
Pittsburgh 2020

Acknowledgments

Grateful acknowledgment is made to the editors of the following publications, in which these poems first appeared:

Alaska Quarterly Review: "Madame Bovary" and "Muta Cupido"; *The Account*: "Rapture" and "Cinéma Vérité"; *The American Journal of Poetry*: "Pilgrimage" and "Revival"; *Bear Review*: "Against Nostalgia"; *Beloit Poetry Journal*: "Theory of Everything"; *Bennington Review*: "The Equivocal World"; *The Best American Poetry blog*: "Guiding Light" and "Meridian"; *Boston Review*: "God Save the Queen"; *carte blanche*: "Arcadian" and "Carpe Noctem"; *The Common*: "Historiae Mundi" and "Homiletic"; *Connotation Press: An Online Artifact*: "Ex Oblivione" and "Threnody"; *Cream City Review*: "Pastoral"; *Diagram*: "Adult Entertainment," "Speaking That Which Leads to Salvation" and "Redundancy, Redundancy"; *Dial2 Magazine*: "Empire"; *Free Verse: A Journal of Contemporary Poetry and Poetics*: "Convolvulus" and "Apocrypha"; *Hobart*: "Rhapsody" and "Res Domestica"; *Horsethief*: "In the Age of Suspect Pleasures," "A Star Is Born" and "The Golden Arches"; *Love's Executive Order*: "I Can't Go On, I'll Go On"; *New Orleans Review*: "Epithalamium"; *Oversound*: "Belle Époque" and "Desideratum"; *Ploughshares*: "Any God Will Do" and "Aubade"; *Queen Mob's Teahouse*: "Matins"; *RHINO*: "Testimony"; *Shenandoah*: "Axis Mundi"; *Tammy*: "Night Shift" and "Pilgrim's Progress"; *32 Poems*: "The Gilded Age"; *THRUSH*: "Tableau Vivant"; *Vinyl Poetry*: "Mon Guerlain"; *Washington Square Review*: "Imagine What a Lifetime Could Do"; *Western Humanities Review*: "La Vie"; *Witness*: "Zeitgeist"; *Yes Poetry*: "Ex Machina" and "I Love Hamburgers"

Profound thanks to Gerald Costanzo, Connie Amoroso, Cynthia Lamb, and the wonderful team at Carnegie Mellon University Press, for supporting this book.

Thank you to my family for all their love and encouragement: James, Theresa, Mark, Carol, Anne, and Bijan.

Thank you to my mentors, friends, and beloveds for reading and inspiring these poems: Cyrus Cassells, Stephen Kampa, John Emil Vincent, Stephanie Bolster, Klara du Plessis, Lesley Trites, Anita Anand, Michelle Syba, Jennifer Moore, Leah Umansky, Bridget Lowe, Caitlyn Doyle, Kathleen Rooney, Kate Greenstreet, Kristina Marie Darling, Tommy Zurhellen, Glenn Shaheen, Wyn Cooper, Nathan McClain, Michelle Livas, Cynthia Mitchell, Brad MacDonald, Eileen G'Sell, Emily Viggiano Saland, Amy Savage, Sarah Giragosian, and Heather Treseler.

Book design by Faith Kim & Connie Amoroso

Library of Congress Control Number 2019953770
ISBN 978-0-88748-653-1
Printed and bound in the United States of America

10 9 8 7 6 5 4 3 2 1

for my family

Contents

Damned is the age that needs heroes.
    —Bertold Brecht

That the impossible should be asked of me, good, what else could be asked of me?
    —Gilles Deleuze

A Star Is Born

Don't mess with a woman
from Texas. No, I'm not
from Texas, but I was raised
by wolves. In saying that, though,
am I appropriating the experience
of those literally raised by wolves,
as I was only using it as a metaphor
for neglect? Whatever. But really,
you're going to do this root canal
without Novocain? I confess:
I like witty people. I credit
them with having overcome
the shittiness of the world.
What is my greatest dream?
To become a jazz pianist,
and see money grow on trees.
It's the getting there that hurts.
It's the getting there that costs
a gazillion dollars, or its
equivalent in virgin tears.
When alone, we are all
Judy Garland, and that is
why I want to be alone.
There is no way to describe
the sublimity of music
entering a room suffering
under a gag rule for years.
If I can learn to do that,
my God, I will have won.

Adult Entertainment

"I got you," the man in the porn
said to the woman in the porn.
Meaning, I won't let you fall.
Literal meaning is a balm;
acts of tenderness can occur
just about anywhere.
To be freed from the burden
of being oneself is a joy
rarer than orchids: a joy
only animals and thespians
know. The world is slated
for liquidation, which is better
than demolition, n'est-ce pas?
"I got you," the man in the porn
said to the woman in the porn.
Meaning, you're not going anywhere,
anytime soon. In another context,
in another poem, *to get* implies
comprehension: a brief elision
between sacrosanct worlds.
I hurl myself against the glass door,
like a spurned employee, or lover.
It won't break. The world has me
in its grip, when all I ever wanted
was to be fucked, then left alone.

Against Nostalgia

I am a master of none, save for
the white mutations of dream.
Items leak from my grasp.
I have a mouth but cannot scream.
Dear compass, dear variorum,
I want the lion's share
of whatever spoils
you deign to drop.
The process is alluvial,
sifting through sediment
to find a saltwater pearl.
In my off-hours, I drowse
behind mosquito netting,
lured on by the metallic moon,
aphrodisiac of oysters and champagne.
This is the fourth state of matter,
storm cloud of senescence threatening
to break and flood the village again.
History is redux: fungus stippling the rock.
Where am I now, you think, now that
you are no longer thought. You come to me
in visions, peeling back the bark of a tree.
Loss and compensation, compensation
and loss. I am healed of indecision.
Do not cast your aspersions on me.

Any God Will Do

If you forget me, remember the Italian ice
we shared in Venice, leaning over a parapet.
I believe it was sour apple. Now, you pluck
a single tulip from the pixelated blizzard,
expecting from me, a Pavlovian response.
In the absence of stimulus, my mind returns
to a paradisiacal state, where I am continually
piqued, but not obligated to produce, or respond.
There are no machine guns, or cameras, here.
If war is what happens when language fails,
I fault the blood sport we became. In lieu
of constancy, doubt. In lieu of variation,
betrayal. What is a word, but an ambition
poorly matched to the task? If you forget
me, remember the summer we holed up
in my threadbare apartment, barely pausing
to do anything but love. It's amazing,
what one will do for warmth. I'm here
to offer, you said, a rational point
of view. Our aptitude for perishing
cannot help but impress, like watching
a supernova or nuclear weapon implode.
Remember me scentless, except when
wearing the Prada perfume you bought me.
We were celebrating the end of illusion,
which is dangerous. We need our dreams.
Lying to my face, after asking you to swear
to god, any god, is how I will remember you.

Apocrypha

At best, life is hard. At worst, life is easy.
I just want to edit out the heartbreaking parts,
screen shot of me on my knees, scouring for change.
Check out the pretty panties on that mannequin.
Check out the sound of ice cubes rattling
in my third whiskey on rocks of the day.
Is that mirror reflecting me? The eighth
mystery of the world is when what is familiar
does not lead automatically to contempt.
Take marriage, for example.
Take the three- and seven-year itch.
I choose you, my escaped convict,
running ragged in the midst.
May someone prepare a hammock
for your body and drooping head.
I miss the church's indulgences, miss
the days of traditional blessings.
Pick up the goddamn phone.
The sun is an education, but
it will be hours until daylight.
May the road rise to meet you,
God-fearing, neutered by labor.
May you not die alone.

Arcadian

I am in love with the way I see the world,
but I am all alone there.

None of this matters.
We make our meek adjustments:

we barter body parts for wine.
All ecstasy is vertiginous.

There are times when I listened
and heard no one saying no.

Learn the errata of the mouth.
Learn the lesson of the pioneer.

O eros, put away your bully stick.
O liberty, put away your crown.

My body does the burning:
it's a kind of winning.

I am the loneliest planet,
a vacancy sign hung askew

at a claptrap, seedy motel:
my flesh is all I know.

You open your mouth wide enough
for me to crawl in and speak.

If there is a place further from me
I beg you do not go.

Ars Poetica

I am not an animal walking in place.
I am not a marble goddess whose breasts
resemble bayonets of spring.
I am a prefatory remark, cast out
in the darkness, an elegy to afterlife.
I am a lost star, careening along the
cosmic Autobahn at the speed
of a broken commuter, or light.
I am not hungry. I have been satiated
on the locust, have had my share
of honey and macadam.
It's true, art makes us other, but I am not
skull candy, an orgasm, nor a wishbone.
I do not exist to make things singsong.
I am not a lever; I can't make it work,
or go. Engineer me, addressee,
out of the earnestness of prose.
Birth the future with forceps.
I know one direction: home.

Aubade

It's an art to suck the marrow
from a bone, a woman
who lived through poverty
once said to me. My own
debt-to-income ratio drives me
to drink, in the afternoon, and
at night. The neon strobe lights
at our favorite club illuminate
your face, before it shutters
and closes off. In the end,
happiness and meaning
are irreconcilable differences,
especially on the dance floor.
I am passionate, of course:
I gesticulate wildly, kneel
before shrines, light candles
that smell of linen in the memory
of my grandparents, and saints,
especially Jude and Lucy,
who had her eyes gouged
out with a hot poker
according to medieval legend.
Meta-cognition takes too long
to explain to those without hearts,
or brains. Last night, you took
my earlobe in your mouth,
teasing out sensations I thought
I was incapable of feeling
until I realized I was.
A friend asked me to lunch,

not realizing I do not eat
lunch. I wake. It is dawn.
As was foretold, I am alone.

Axis Mundi

Heart of my innermost doll-child;
heart of petit fours on a tray;
you are a bonfire upon which
children spit, waiting for their ride
back from the Museum of Science
and Industry, where they espy
an interactive coal mine, and
the U505 submarine, on display.
Upstart heart, totemic crow.
We await your circumspect vows.
We acknowledge your slow bleed.
We demand to know, are we the chosen:
will we be present when you're crowned
Queen of Nuclear Fallout, secret weapon
of the late empire's last lovers, détente.

Belle Époque

My life is a rerun commercial
of two men clinking beers.
I cross and recross
my legs, observe the
slow persistence of bugs
making their way across
walls, the Western plain.
Blush was created to simulate
sexual arousal, and mascara,
the doe-eyed gaze of youth.
I must be tripping. I am tripping,
on the red carpet between preface
and coda, anarchy of a bygone
era that may not have actually
happened. Why trust historians
when you have hyperarousal,
a leashed mutt, at your side?
I can't not give everything,
but then I run up against
the problem of time.
I only want that which
is forbidden; I hate
miserliness like I
hate toxic oil spills
in the Aegean Sea.
What rhymes with you
but the idea of ardor?
Winds of change, Ides
of March: deliver me.

Carpe Noctem

Because the veil was lifted.
Because the dog has rabies.
Because the soul sleepwalks into a mirror
and our desire is increased by difficulty.
Because disappointment is an obstacle,
like longing, like fate.
Because I died young and beautiful.
Because I will not die young and beautiful.
Because mother tongue, motherland, mother lode.
Because peace offering. Small pittance. Precious geode.
Because the domesticated animal is exhausted,
drapes its limp body across a stretch of cement.
Because I don't want to historicize my feelings.
Because without the world's innumerable
fungal varieties, we'd be fucked,
as without fungi, we'd soon be
knee-deep in dead leaves that
refused to rot: trees, too,
would lie where they fell.
Because crops would fail
and farm animals die,
unable to digest grass.
Because outside, the magnolia is in bloom.
There will be no restitution,
because I could not stop for death.
Because what you wanted, I wanted that for you.

Cinéma Vérité

Should Nature be my profile photo
or my cover photo? Should I adopt
a mantra or tantra? Must I again face

a heckling crowd, or a bad steward
of the earth whipping the one animal
entrusted to him? If so, kill me now.

Actually, I think I am already dead.
My brain is floating in formaldehyde;
my preferred pastime is staring at the wall.

But I am godlike at the typewriter, and I am
also a skilled movie critic; when the subtitles
or voice-overs are off, I know instantly.

If brevity is the soul of wit, I am clearly soulless,
as I take forever to say anything, or get anywhere,
despite the ministrations of multiple seraphim:

it takes an army to keep me alive. I no longer fear
mirrors, because I know who I am looking at; I am,
surprise surprise, looking at me. Jesus Christ,

Superstar, are you just going to stand there and
watch me burn? I pegged you as one who preferred
a story to an anecdote, but clearly I was mistaken.

My sails are set for Death Valley, despite the flat
foreground and financial exigencies of today.
See above. See below. Move the decimal,

I mean decibel, two places to the left: then
you'll know my worth, my value, my market share.
Love is a pocketful of kryptonite, extemporaneous

words spoken in the heat of passion, off the cuff.
You knew me; I knew you. Let that be enough.

Clair de Lune

Who said the novel is a vaudeville show,
the six o'clock news, the mumblings
of wild men saddled by demons?
I want to give you everything:
lavish banquets, valuable books,
suits made out of horsehair and twine.
I want to give you the coronal sublime.
If I speak for the dead, I must leave
this animal of my body,
denatured unto dust.
The moon is in her stirrups
and the doctor's prognosis is time.
Lay yourself on the tarmac;
ignore the buzzards of air.
Alien geometries may speak
in vile tongues but you,
a perfect storm, will prevail.

Convolvulus

Ghosts are not empty, nor are they sad.
They are parenthetical asides, bodiless,
with tiny outstretched hands. So what
if your eyes are the color of indigo ink,
your form the mold into which cement
is poured, then cools? Sunset is archetypal,
which makes it no less real. Anthophilous,
this landfill crisis isn't going to go away
on its own. Have you seen that gargantuan
pile of abandoned tires? How quickly
passion becomes nostalgia, twining plant
with trumpet-shaped flowers, many of which
are invasive weeds. Go ahead, keep bragging.
I am not above throwing money at the problem,
but I have no money to throw at the problem, and
strategic disrobing is not a solution. For example,
you asked for an image of me, so I sent you
a photo of my body, you wrote back, upset,
saying what you wanted was a photo of my face.
I wanted to give you something beautiful,
metaphor not as decoration but thought,
say, but you rejected my dry goods store.
I love love, its tenderness and cruelty,
hypnagogic ode to what will be no more.

Desideratum

Lies, like sugarplums,
dance through my head.
Like a heroine stabbed
to death in an opera,
my sciatica nerve
flares, then subsides,
before flaring up again.
Is a crime only a crime
if one is caught? Synesthesia
is for the charmed among us,
those capable of moving
between love and loathing,
or merely moving at all.
The last emoji on the list
of emojis is a country flag:
long may she wave, or reign.
I like it in my opium den.
It's warm, quiet, and dank;
I smoke until my poker face
falls flat on the marble floor.
My human desire is simple:
to live on the perpetual cusp
of extremity, hour between
disbelief and ecstasy, having
been, and to be forevermore.

Election Day

To find a form that accommodates the mess
one must dive deep into shell-shocked shores,
past the shallows, into the heart of the wreck.
There you will find the ruins of civilization,
obliterated husk of symphonic wholes.
Listen: the tinny music from the pleasure
boat is still carried by the wind.
There, there. I will cloak you with the
solicitude of centuries; I will write
on your body with the squid ink
of uncertainty. This land is your land.
This land is my land. This land
belongs to the exorable animals
we've attempted to eliminate—
buffalo, wolves—and to the
dispossessed. There is no largesse
enough to accommodate
the terror you feel. Pull up a chair.
Take a number. Amazing
grace, how sweet the sound,
of the roulette wheel.

Empire

Color shocks,
like the invention of penicillin.
Who am I to be bled in this way?
We make inroads in discourse,
interventions, and the like,
while in neighboring countries
body parts are auctioned
and punishment meted out
according to fallible law.
So much depends upon
the right words in the right order,
not just spoken in mutiny,
but also propinquity.
This vodka, for example,
is made of bison grass
and can be applied to wounds.
Draw closer. I have distilled
the literal. You can touch it—
the idea within the thing, metaphor.

Epithalamium

I ask you to help me move
the cadaver: you demure.
I ask you to help me conjugate
French verbs: you aver.
I ask you for the sun & moon,

to rewrite the dictionary,
to decolonize modern love.
I ask your help in coming
of age, with middle age,
with contractions

and police records.
I ask you to preserve me
from officialdom, to
wait for hours while
I paint my face and set my hair.

I want the pure thought, unchained,
smallest units of language
conspiring to become other
as they balance, like
molecules of air.

Ex Machina

God, seduction is such a bore.
I fall asleep at the control panel

of the Tilt-A-Whirl. I can see
you're having fun, which is great,

but the only thought I'm having is:
ramp it up, ramp it down, then go.

The problems of suffering and desire
are not about forbearance or delayed

gratification. It's about identifying
the one hurdle you've identified as

insurmountable, then mounting it.
Ta-da. Voilà. So there. With you,

anything seemed possible. What do
you mean, I don't have to put my

toiletries in travel-size containers?
Do you surmount the jurisdiction

of airport security, too? So long.
Thanks for the retirement luncheon,

the gold watch you set ticking like a
bat out of hell, when what I really

wanted was a diamond tennis bracelet,
pay-per-view, and a chubby child

to call my own. The wicked prosper.
Everyone is a tourist, sometimes.

I make up for deceit in innovation,
in being willing to sacrifice a lung.

Every subject needs its object: mine,
a bell so heavy it cannot be rung.

Ex Oblivione

I have reached the end
of my ability to troubleshoot.
I have reached the end
of my fantasy life, mélange
of magical thinking
and exegesis of sin.
In calligraphy, if a stroke falters,
you must begin the word all over again.
Glory be to Inanna,
ancient Mesopotamian goddess
associated with beauty, love, and war.
It's true, I am bored stiff.
It's true, there is a residue
of velum in my mouth.
O sexless being,
desire is god's fingerprint.
The body does not want to be a spectacle.
The body does not want to be a blood sport.
I am picturing the parts of a camera.
I am picturing momentum,
the periodic table, a one-night stand.
Zero is a real number:
arousal an ululation in the throat.
I am picturing myself caught
in flagrante delicto, unashamed.
Give me a poem without suffering,
Lord. Give me your outstretched hand.

Fire Sermon

We stood and watched the flames lick the amphitheater,
the library, the multimillion-dollar sports complex.

I understood metaphor the first time I heard
a house's antechambers described as wings.

Empire is a scalar model of an antique train.
Circle and circles of infinite regression and delay.

The fire ate the firehouse, the firemen,
and the concept of causality.

We stood in our rubber waders,
catastrophically underdressed.

But there was no fire, in the end,
only a poem about fire.

The fire had a terminus,
as did the metaphor, the train.

Fugue

It's incredible what one
can do with a quiver
of arrows, if one's
intentions are correct.

I make a voodoo doll
of my enemies, whom
I am told to love with
a godly love.

For every person you delight,
there are three people
you are letting down.
May the odds be ever

in your favor. May the
sun shine warmly on your back.
Don't hide your light under
a bushel, said Jesus.

As if we had a light to hide.
I cross myself, twice.
I was born to believe.
I let the arrows fly.

God Save the Queen

Dear Media State and your
concomittant buzzfeed,

I am, how you say, done.
Done drama. Done infomerical.

Done cortisone shot to the brain.
Done *General Hospital*, done

As the World Turns, done *Days
of Our Lives*, done horse dung,

Daddy Warbucks, and speed.
Where, Pentacostal Lord,

is my acre to hoe, my tiara,
my land of honeyed mead?

Self-portrait in a concave mirror:
late for my own funereal destiny.

Three little birds on my doorstep.
The last tree standing, in Calvary.

Guiding Light

I wasted my life on language
and other soft constructions,
held the clammy hand of death
as if death was the snot-nosed kid
last to be picked for any team
where skill actually matters.
I could be a bride, and was,
was bridled, harnessed, and
groomed. Now I live in, and by,
a burning timetable, abetting
the landfill crisis by buying
ream after ream of paper.
The bright white paper.
The laser paper.
The paper whose opacity
rivals that of God.
I indicate I would like
the dessert menu by pointing to it
with my bony finger.
When it comes, I order a financier.
As the World Turns, I remain still,
Mona Lisa's resting bitch face
blunted only by my silky curtain of hair.
Throw it all in the cauldron, I don't care.
People keep mistaking me for a doll
when in fact I am a cyborg,
surrounded by *The Young & the Restless*
snorting coke and drinking corpse revivers
in the *General Hospital*—downward,

I mean backward, glance of Orpheus
softening my every blow.
My fantasy for this script is simple:
I just want to edit out the boring parts,
the parts where I forgot to scream.
Guiding Light is my real life:
the world around me is the dream.

Helen Keller Confesses All

I once threw kings, like toy soldiers,
off the map of the world. Two-dimensional
in my eyes, empire could be yanked
like a tablecloth from a table,
preserving only the original frame.
Now I know what others have suffered
from me, for I burn with the love
of my own self. . . . Only death
can set me free, saith Narcissus,
to himself. Being blind is like that.
Yet the more a work costs,
the greater the status it confers.
Is dysfunction and difference
a commodity value, or cachet?
Lord, I am concerned about
the sumptuary value of the soul.
How it's constructed, and undone
by acts of language: atomic bomb
of the noun and the verb.

Helen Keller's Eternal Flame

Humming a song that hasn't yet been invented,
he is standing at the foot of my bed,
certain parts of his body missing, as if erased
with Wite-Out in a final draft of a student thesis
on the Industrial Revolution or the Scientific Method,
as applied to aesthetics, or porn. Let us go now,
you and I, into a dub-step remix of a bee-loud glade,
I thought I heard him say. As in every beginning,
I counted out the syllables in my palm, traced
the letters of his name on my thigh. *We'll vacation
in Reykjavik*, he said, *live in an igloo, and swoon.*
He speaks 14 languages. His eyes gleam.
He has never been married, until now.

Helen Keller at the Rodeo

To despair is to no longer have
experiences, except the idea thereof—
to be cosseted in a black cape,
immune to both sights and sounds.
It's watching you watch the matador
taunt the bull with the Veronica maneuver,
the self-same motion of a woman of faith,
who wiped the face of Jesus while he walked
to Calvary. Lord, we all crave release,
be it at the ring in Cheyenne, Wyoming,
or along Orchard Road, in Singapore.
The world is a welter of homonyms.
How does one finally arrive, get born?
I am writing your name as if I were a Trojan
who expected someone else to smooth the shore.

Helen Keller in Antibes

In my seeing there was a blank and he filled that blank
with words: lighthouse, absinthe, Côte d'Azur, reverb.
He carved a space in the gray matter of my brain, asked:
what is lithium, but a siphoning of the voltage of mind?
We worked the crossword: *amour propre, amour fou.*
Only idiots, French or otherwise, I said,
willingly engage in a *folie à deux.*
Pas de retour. Loup garou. I taught
him the footwork of Isadora Duncan:
the melancholic strains of Beethoven's
late string quartets, composed in his
Third Period, when he was entirely deaf.
I want to outsmart death, he whispered.
Myself, I said, *I want to outsmart you.*

Historiae Mundi

Life on the hillside of the Euphrates:
a star in the process of exploding.
In the shadowy interstice between
language and anguish, I stand, sketching
silhouettes of the soul's four dimensions,
while androids dream of electric sheep.
Money isn't nothing: nor is it substance,
life. O wanton superlative, isn't it ironic,
I mean iconic, I mean ionic, that the opposite
of obfuscation is transparency? As if I could
even see five feet in front of me. As if the x axis
and the y axis, accordant and discordant, could
ever converge. The brain inhibits one from
engaging in dangerous activities—google it!—
but that part of the brain can be overwritten.
Sad to say, the literary industrial complex is
unstoppable, endless precincts of nightmare
populated by denizens of popular taste.
To argue otherwise is futile. To argue
otherwise is to carve a small cave within
a cave, a space where one can breathe
despite the meaninglessness of bodies.
If I delete all images and texts of yours,
do you then cease to exist? Voilà, a boundary.
Voici, my soul, a unified design concept.
Gird your loins, guard your last red cent:
the executioner's song is a madrigal.
The executioner's song is all assent.

Homiletic

Nothing is analogous to God.
In order to strike, a cobra also needs
to recoil. All good things, and strokes
of bad luck, happen in threes,
and so let it be this way with us:
from lust, to neutrality, to disgust.
Let me tell you a different story.
I am asking for forgiveness for buying
stock in high proof liquor, for making
eyes at the neighborhood gnome.
Evolution: the identification of a need,
the fulfillment of a need. Daylight
ends, and we agree not to call this
a tragedy. I dismount this life
like a gymnast from a vault:
valorously, without pride.
The opposite of loneliness is
the shared illusion of intimacy.
The opposite of an algorithm
is the futility of awakened desire.
So what if all being is hypothetical?
You took the last of my imagined
grief, and left me with fire.

I Can't Go On, I'll Go On

Dear potentate. If we don't have a word for something,
do we then spend our whole lives searching for that word?
In Kraków, I climbed the hill to Wawel Castle, alone.
In Budapest, I climbed the hill to Buda Castle, alone.
It's pitiful, the narrativization of experience: life reduced
to sound bites and hashtags, to grabby phrases and self-
aggrandizing anecdotes. Dear Bullmastiff, we love
to flatter ourselves, and others. We preen in reflective
surfaces like children discovering depth perception.
Beyond the I, the I. I have spent my life searching
for a word that I cannot, will not, know. Something
to do with the exhaustion of the possible, enchantment,
desire, and an unwillingness to breed. Dear mentor,
Dear mentee, what's the point of consciousness, if
it's always at heel? We're so completely screwed,
no matter what I say or don't say, no matter whether
ideas are learned or remembered, is my current theory
on aesthetics and the problem—aren't they all—of God.
I get up, drink coffee, watch animal rescue videos
before reentering the slog, the drill, the grind.
As the Eagles say, take it to the limit, one more time.

I Love Hamburgers

As Thich Nhat Hanh said, you should not say
I love hamburgers, as love is a sacred word
that should be reserved for the flesh, or soul.
I am afraid of Virginia Woolf, as I discovered
what black magic can do. Can't stop won't stop.
Noah's Ark, as we know, was built for two.
I know I'm forgetting something, such as
a good-night kiss, which I cannot render
as it would irreparably fuck up my lipstick.
I can no longer afford my hovercraft, now
that the sale of diesel has skyrocketed again.
Yes, Fräulein, give me another one of your
pietistic platitudes about sex and grammar
and the grammar of sex. Give me the life
wisdom of bean counters who ascribe genius
to photosynthesis in the Darkest Age.
O, to be a diva, so fucking special that
not a single person could ever forget
the tread of your footstep on their face.
You want to know the secret to victory?
Dance like no one is watching, even though
everyone is watching. Tell me: is it so bad
to desire desire in perpetuity? And here's
God again. Stuck in the deep web with you.

Imagine What a Lifetime Could Do

Hell, in all religions, is hot:
infernal region slash netherworld
where the quixotic lure of pheromones
leads us to self-destruct time and time
again. I do not know how it came to pass
that you and I were pressed up against
each other in a broom closet, but maybe
that was just the machinations of destiny.
Have you ever had someone kiss your
bandaged wound? It's amazing.
It's like being set loose in a zoo.
You asked for a picture of me,
so I drew you a misshapen heart
in a concave mirror, going up in flames.
When am I not going up in flames?
Here, you will find me, combing the ash
for a good tooth or two. In a biblical play,
I would be cast not as Mary, but Hagar,
Egyptian handmaid and surrogate mother
to the world. Our Lady of Perpetual Whatever,
and whores, please come swiftly, through
that narrow door marked *SORTIE*.
The likelihood of the rich being
able to enter heaven is steadily
decreasing, as is the width of
the eye of the proverbial needle.
The book of Genesis is so right on.
On our third day together, we found
dry land, green grass, and fruit.
Imagine what a lifetime could do.

In the Age of Suspect Pleasures

All our pleasures seem suspect these days.
The lion jumping through the burning hoop
at the now-defunct circus was trained
with bull hooks, as lions are inherently
afraid of fire. The word *natural*:
the feeling one gets when high
on speed, or its equivalent—
I can conquer the world.
Then comes the severed cords
of the marionette: your best
a chthonic hallucination, in vain.
Reading trashy fiction, starring
a fireman and his hose. Eating
pain au chocolat until dopamine
begins its slow drip in your brain.
I can't express to you enough, the
letter begins. *La tristesse durera
toujours*, it ends. Enough with
deconstruction, its meager fruits.
I shred the book into pieces.
I wheel the dolly down the hall.
O, for a death to end death.
Is springtime folly? Pagan
mysteries—like gathering
a god's remains—unite us all.

In the Late Style of Eros

Loneliness is a female shark
who circles the tank repeatedly,

feigning interest in aesthetics,
before finally eating the male.

The pleasure's in not yielding
to mere lust, or despair.

Why bother telling you
you look like a man I loved,

when in fact you are that man,
or at least were, in the

Pleistocene era of big hair?
Four score and ten minutes ago

I looked at your photograph,
so proud to know you,

as if you were my famous relative
when in fact you're the stranger next door.

O, mealymouthed cliché.
O, sweet-smelling catastrophe.

Welcome to our life
before it was lived,

dust-bowl epic eliciting
no feeling but awe.

La Vie

The slot where the milk bottles
used to flow freely at the house
of my grandmother in Old Brooklyn,
a neighborhood of Cleveland
densely populated by Polish
and Slovenian immigrants,
is now sealed shut. This is the hour
of lead, milk replaced by the venom
of exotic serpents. Scratch that.
Quotidian serpents, bottom-feeders
who rise to wealth and power
through exploitation and lies.
I can fly, we said as kids,
cape fluttering as we stood
at the helm of the boat,
if we were lucky enough
to know someone with a boat.
Life with its trembling wraith
and prewar memorabilia.
Life with its sorrow, its bleed.
Imagination, invagination:
both need seed money.
Had we but world
enough, and time.
Life with its rugged cross,
its whimper, its need.

Madame Bovary

an erasure of *Madame Bovary* by Gustave Flaubert,
translated by Lydia Davis

Look at those pretty daisies. Oracles enough
for any village girl who happens to be in love.
Why rant against the passions? Aren't they the only
beautiful thing on earth, the source of heroism,
enthusiasm, poetry, music, the arts?
How bored I am! How bored I am!
A surgeon's caresses are like the oil with which
he greases his scalpel. When I lost my poor dear
late lamented, I would go into the fields to be all alone;
I would fling myself down under a tree, I would weep.
He liked hard cider, a rare leg of lamb, *glorias* well beaten.
She would think of all the wild emotions, unknown to her.
Why hadn't she seized that happiness when it was offered?
She would end by asking him to give her some tonic
for her health, and a little more love.
Would this misery last forever?
She grew pale and had palpitations of the heart.
At other times, burning hotly with that secret flame,
she would open her window, breathe in the cold air,
and, looking at the stars, long for princely loves.
You're ungodly! You have no religion!
A convulsion flung her back on the mattress.
Here I am, I'm yours.

Mata Hari at L'Heure Exquise

After the lobotomy, they scraped my brain
cavity like a child rustling up
the last bite of ice-cream from a bowl.
All done. All gone. *All good.*

Firing squad, I am a free-floating agent,
stripped from the putrescence of memory,
delivered into spellbinding feature films
without reason, adjectives, or nouns.

My heart's hot tears smart
and spatter on my shirt
like blood from a fattened lamb.
I laugh at my own histrionics.

Look who's laughing now.
O, lyric subjectivity.
O, exotic German spy.
Who knew you could quell a crowd?

My mind is an odorless vapor.
My soul's fire-fangled feathers
wrangle five-star smiles.
I, Robot. I, Claudius. I bow.

Matins

God's business model sucks.
Thus, God's a man after my own heart.
He'd rather sit in a plastic chair at a
Midwestern bowling alley, yelling
STRIKE to those whose balls belong
to the gutter. Why, you ask?
Well shit, why are you asking me?
You think I have a moral compass?
I'll steal anything not nailed down,
including park benches and certified mail.
Dear diversified portfolio, this flesh wound
is arterial: this sleeping bag, built for one.
You came back to earth full of desire, deranged monster
who forgot other people existed beside you. Atypical,
atypical: there is no reason in your theory of life,
no fruit at all, in fact. You can't force me
to quit, surrender, or forfeit the game, and
I don't care if we run out of metaphors
while partying on the manicured lawn.
Someone, somewhere, is ripping your
portrait off the wall. I hope they knife it.
I am a specimen in quarantine, where
I dream the good dream of singular meaning,
poisoned arrow flying into the red eye of dawn.

Meridian

I've been in this body so long.
My ace in the hole body, my one
bird in two hands body, my rut.
What does it mean to understand?
I count the syllables on my hand. I don
my leisure suit and stroll the boardwalk.
O bituminous coal. O indiscriminate
hulk. My Ikea bookshelf body
is flanked by equine statuettes.
The world is full of tall strangers
and I haven't seen a face
that loves me for days.
O moon, you are a hangnail.
O moon, your hair's a fright.
Note bene, this product has been
enlarged to show texture.
The cure's a subtle realignment
between one's inner monster
and the line of longitude that scores
the earth. I thought beauty would
save me. No, I really thought
beauty would save me.
I've been in this body so long;
I've forgotten how to flee.
Objects in the mirror may
be closer than they appear:
they too ache with unknown
want, dumb weight of destiny.

Mon Guerlain

I once had a thirst for knowledge.
Now I deseed jalapenos for their
immersion in tequila. What is this
flawed obedience. What is this
strange obsequy. I am searching
for my threshold. I am trying not
to confuse a Trojan horse with
pyrrhic victory. I have forgotten
how to hyphenate, how to ventilate.
My twin lung sacks have wilted,
like roses given on the occasion
of *I'm sorry, please forgive me,*
before the offender strikes again.
If I could just visit Bora Bora.
If I could just find my
signature perfume.
Yesterday, we argued
about which gunshot wounds
are fatal. Seems best, we concluded,
to avoid the major arteries, heart,
and brain. I dream of confluence,
the junction of two rivers, but
my dream is always ruined
by the reality of effluent.
Dogged, you pursue me,
to the point of no return.

Muta Cupido

Go ahead, erase the source text.
My only desire: to feel the sun,
that pimp, on my etiolated form.
I am famished. I understand the face
value of beauty, but that doesn't stop me
from dying for it. O killdeer, unsex me.
Invent an allegory for restitution, peace.
Yes, I crashed into a retention wall,
seeking news of you. I can't believe
I survived. If death is a time warp,
what is life? This is forgiveness, redacted.
This is a surge of syllables, dangling
from my mouth. I was born to deadhead
the peonies. I was born, like medieval art,
to degrade. Domini, domini, I chose breadth
over depth. I chose to offer nothing remedial
or heartwarming to the world. Mary stands still,
benign in blue, plastic arms outstretched.
Or is that polyurethane? Her dress flares
at the knee, as if prepared for a Roman holiday.
I have no sense of what this means to you,
save one lit glimpse of how we live,
a more expansive sense in whom.
I am an atheist who says her prayers,
a little world made cunningly,
a parcel of vain strivings, tied.
I am a poor nun of perpetual adoration
who confuses streetlamps for the moon.

Night Shift

Do you know Excel? We need a spreadsheet,
a game plan, a modus operandi that actually
fucking works, in the vast vomitorium
that is the failed dream of progress.
Greco-Roman culture, you gave birth
to Hellenism and coliseums, temples
in the Doric, Ionic, and Corinthian styles,
but what has become of your virility?
I look to the constellations, stars like
punch holes in the sky. A little light
dribbles through. I couldn't catch it.
Hence, demotion. Hence, underemployment
and imposter syndrome in the land of vendettas.
I'm so sick of syntax, of feigned elan. I am lost
in the underwood between sentence and sentience,
unafraid of gravity's siren song. Put away your
bully stick, already. I'm just going to sit here,
stoically, until gripped by otherworldly feeling.
When it doesn't come, I'll turn on you like a
junkyard dog. Pity us our impotence, God.
Pity us, we have no one to whom to belong.

Pastoral

It's almost autumn. Gen Z
adjusts its headphones,

for the sound of Chance
the Rapper to come booming through.

Remind me who's a fickle mistress:
is it Nature, or Time?

I'm no prophet.
I knew my friend's marriage

was doomed when she told me
her husband said: what's yours is mine,

and what's mine is mine.
Idiocy comes in three colors.

Insanity is measured by degrees.
Whoever said the devil is in the details

knew a thing or two
about assembling furniture, or disease.

The only known paradise beckons,
stupor of five-dollar margaritas

and slot machines. It was a mistake
to anthropomorphize the mascot.

It was a mistake to mistake
for lumber, the trees.

Phantom Limb

This is what the portrait says:
I'm trying not to eviscerate the word.
Here is an animal, a perimeter.
Here is the golden ratio
between muscle memory and God.
I long for your embrace.
I brace myself for your longing.
I'm not myself most mornings,
avidity a lozenge on my tongue.
I cross myself.
I hex myself.
I wear the most forgettable
eau de parfum.
Dear metastatic metaphor:
distance, too, is proportional.
If I was a soldier in the forest,
I would think twice.
If I were a flattened angel,
my body would uncurl like clouds.
I just want an immersive experience.
There are only so many stories: maybe 12.
I have the voice of someone who sucked on helium.
I have the voice of someone moving at the speed of light.
Life is a gift, it's true, one easily swapped for another.
A pitchfork, say, or gun.
That is the way with amputations:
blood rushing, blood pooling, blood gone.

Pilgrimage

Gather your things. Gather thy thou.
All aboard the train to nowhere,
where we will be guided by a weather vane,

a freak show, a nun. Allow the passenger
pigeons to pass. This life is an intoxicant,
which can be traded for another substance

less heady, champagne bubbles
rising like the dew point of hysteria.
Here in the white room, we will

decide between illness as metaphor
and metaphor as illness. All stimuli
will be first analyzed, then denied.

I implore you to remember the ocean,
the Great Barrier Reef. Holy unrest,
the eighth wonder of the world.

The longing to be pure is over.
I stand along the promontory,
looking out, like a B actress,

on the great horizon
at the unseen white whale,
the philosopher's stone.

I interrupt my programming
to say something original.
Show me the way to go home.

Pilgrim's Progress

You touched my callused trigger finger
and I felt sensations for the first time
in years. There is no hunger like
sexual hunger, no tears like those
provoked by the skin of an onion,
peeling back layers of performance
until all that's left is a body bereft
of mind. My teeth chatter, in this
antechamber. My fallback plan
is style. Is this anguish, or ennui?
I want to return to my senses. I want
to return to the stage. What is the
circus but a dream of permanence,
spectacle's beginning at the end?
I lowered myself from the ceiling.
I ordered the replacement part but it
never came. Fuck that noise, you said,
but seriously, what master do you serve?
I am lit. I am a sack of confectioner's
sugar, a papier mâché lantern going up
in flames at the wedding of a couple
who will divorce within the year.
But wasn't the cake fantastic,
the bride, an absolute doll?
Extinguish this fire in the
earth's alleged molten core.
Quote how much it will cost
to fix me, and I'll pay it, now.
What else are ovaries, blood,
a soul, and two kidneys for.

Rapture

Lordy Lordy, check out this amphitheater:
there's so much oxygen, I can't even breathe.
And yet I noticed the performance has been
divvied up into ever-shorter time intervals.
What's with that? Do you not trust the span
of our attention, or is this a question of form?
When you referred to the architecture of the idea,
however, I had to laugh. Catechism taught me
I am the price tag on a priceless piece of art.
Let's get rid of the mannequins in the mall,
with their cold plastic nudity, and immobile,
neutered sex. Better to be an other-directed
idiot, like the misshapen moon, or a brutish
prick, mirror reflecting you back to me at
twice your natural size. I used to be ardent,
used to break any window in sight if what
I desired was visible from the other side.
Now, I take melatonin to treat malnutrition,
but there is no pill for this sinking sensation.
Embalmed by the memory of your touch,
I wreak havoc with the trajectory of stars.
My modus operandi is auto-renewing,
yet I've grown rusty without god, child
prodigy at the art of wasting, killing time.
Can't you recognize an appreciating stock?
I put a spell on you, because you're mine.

Redundancy, Redundancy

The operator is tired. The good
wife is tired. It is tiring, to love
grunge rock, only to have it fly
in the face of established taste
time and time again. Time and time
again, I dream of French classics
(onion soup and short ribs), though
I have not eaten meat in years.
It's something about that sidewalk
café, newspaper ruffling in the wind
like a Dead Sea Scroll, murmuration
of Parisians eating their daily bread.
When painters surrender their right
to title their own paintings, strange
things happen. Weird blob No. 4.
Amorphous postindustrial landscape
No. 2. I would like to start this life
over again, in media res. I would
like to cut your heart out with a spoon.
I am uncomfortable with directionals,
with the exception of true north.
I am uncomfortable with imperatives,
with the exception of Go away.
I live on the cliff face of whatever
mountain I happen to be scaling.
Starling, darling: the pain of
nonexistence is continual.
Come closer. Drink deeper.
Die another day.

Res Domestica

Who will make me a mere body again?
The trick is to hollow yourself out
until nothing is left but form.
Come over to my anthropod
and we'll make passionate love
atop a toy carousel,
with lacquered horses
going round and round.
It's propitious weather
to become a human turnstile.
The salt water laps
at the wind-beaten prow.
The bromide of evening thins,
wears out. We're left hanging
onto banisters, our voices
a mere scratch on the turntable.
Charlatan comforts: this room, this chair.
What I meant when I said
one blossom desires the air.

Revival

Poem as penance, straw man.
Poem as ineluctable stain.
Against the high tide of not yet
comes the underground current
of always already here.
The desire is for repetition,
pattern formation. The desire
is that you'd carry the albatross
while I sun momentarily
in the abyss, like a decorated
soldier. So much depends upon
the brain, upshot of intelligence
being the way an erudite sentence
snakes through the mind before
coming to rest—or is it pose—gently
on a promontory. Just for effect.
Just to test the imported liquor
of style and subjectivity. Because
it's un-American not to smile
for the cameras, wave your flag.
Poem as antibiotic, virus, strain.
We'll never reach the summit.
We'll never, like this, be born again.

Rhapsody

I opened the window so I could hear people.
But all I heard was the wind rushing,
fine garment of nothingness, like tulle.
You sent me a handout listing various
cognitive distortions, including
personalization and emotional reasoning,
and let me tell you, it was a scream.
I believe in the dream of human
perfectability, however much
a vista, like mecca, out of reach.
In the meantime I have mastered
the art of appreciating objects
such as marble, which remains
cool even in sweltering heat,
even if objects are nothing more
than the decision of atoms
to remain united in the face
of travesty, poverty, war.
In the meantime I have picked
up several musical instruments
then gently laid them down.
Can you imagine being lucky
enough to devote your life
to French pastries,
working tirelessly to form
stiff peaks of meringue?
There are omens to show you
you are dying. The world
is too much with us, first
as footnote, then as song.

Saint Justine

Sir, I withdraw my ideological investment in your master plan
of concubines, whipping, hot wax, and love-lies-weeping, slain.
This is my letter of resignation from Château de Lacoste.
Thank you for your studious attention to my moral
progress in the House of Corrections. I am a
newborn soul. Now, I am taking myself and my
still-intact virgin forest, despite defenestration,
away. Callow? Naïve? Game? I accept
the natural order and entropic fallout
of things, which you confuse with disdain.
I want the collected works of Jeremy Bentham.
I want a wardrobe of intimate apparel spun from
silkworms, a hot rod and a bubble gum machine.
How do I define heaven? An open field
in which you neither exist, nor reign.

Speaking That Which Leads to Salvation

We speak to remind ourselves
of a vision anterior to this one:
the world's paltry sum. We speak
to raise, if not the dead, then the
swamp life of dreams: pie cooling
on a windowsill; scenic campground;
old yellow dog loping into the arms
of his young hirsute owner. Stay with
the feeling, my counselor once urged me.
Stay with your attraction to the hirsute man,
even if you created him for the sake of singing.
We speak for pleasure's sake, liquid asset
of forethought running off the tongue.
We speak to enumerate our laurels and our
losses: to obviate, deflect, compensate,
and deny. If we are trapped within a one-
room cabin, speech is the rain that pelts
the windowpane, drizzling, steadily,
down. We speak the dream of logos:
wind in a void, communicative
intent, song of the open door.
The third practice in the Noble
Eightfold Path is to speak
that which leads to salvation.
If you have not yet mastered
free indirect discourse, try merging
the character and narrator once more.

Tableau Vivant

Let me tell you about my marvelous god.
He is a landscape in which I play the moving tree.
Slack as a victim in a Victorian novel,
I carry a notebook to record what was said
in the interstice between hope and futility.
I am rowing to you on the great, dark ocean,
said Caravaggio. The internet may just be
the closest I'll ever get to a kind of intimacy.
I wave my foam finger at the sporting event,
hope you'll notice me in this mélange of fans.
I hold my own body, in lieu of someone else
holding it. The smaller one is, the greater the
likelihood of being loved. In the near-eternity,
all metaphors are exact, and when the doctor asks
where it hurts, I don't hesitate. Right here. Here.
Within: the unborn. Without: bodies dashing
through the rain. I wanted to redouble my
efforts, but the primary effort was in vain.
Call me darling, call me dear. Drag me
by my legs, like a baby born breech,
into a higher atmosphere.

Testimony

The day's preamble is this.
You are my hollow, my
absentee ballot, my lake.
Sorrow is my dry goods store.
Bedazzlement keeps us awake.
In the evening, I listen to the
lowing of cows. In the thick of it,
the blue-veined breast of it,
the moon does nothing but yield.
It's said grief is a private matter:
I say joy is the real lone wolf,
a Yellowstone park ranger
in khaki, answering to no one
but the sun and field.

The Equivocal World

If Jesus is the answer, what is the question?
Voulez-vous mourir avec moi?
Psycho killer, *que est ce que ç'est?*

Bed as tribulation. Bed as poplar tree,
barrel of apples, garden created ex nihilo.
Honestly, it's a miracle anything gets made,

let alone all and sundry: what I'm looking at,
now. Hand me my physic, my wire monkey
mother, my spittoon, my vice. Instead of

a musical note, a hole. Instead of a prelude,
desecration. I go to the things I love with no
thought of duty or pity: likewise, the glittery

object in the tall native grass. If I had enough
money to buy a consonant, I would buy a diphthong,
a dent, a disaster. As it is, I am disloyal, mute.

The hysteric and the killjoy move as one.
The bridal party and the bride move as one.
I didn't come here to pay homage to a metonym

for dick, yet I do want the quick and dirty version
of everything, from intelligence briefs to literature.
Why are the most exhausted people I meet described

as tireless by their peers? Why is truth thrice
removed from art? I don't need a curse or vendetta.
I need a primate, versed in deceit, to gift me its heart.

The Gilded Age

The sky is all eyelid
and the moon is a whorl of cotton candy
with no one left to eat it but god.
When happiness comes back,
it comes back on stilts,
on acid, on bended knee.
Like a prodigal. Like a madrigal.
Like a boss man, gold chains glinting
in the harsh September sun.
Fate isn't just an ocean.
Some days aren't worth repeating.
I planted you in the fecund earth
then waited a season for you to bloom.
Shut eye. Hard bulb.
Vituperous species of regret.
You want for nothing: I want a window
beyond me, myself, and me.
Downriver is the past.
Downriver is the foghorn
that used to call the ship to port,
and which now announces
an empty womb, insolvency.

The Golden Arches

Yes, I say yes to the future.
I say yes to the swim-up
tiki bar, drag goddesses,
and pristine theodicy.
Fucking Facebook.
You brandish your ugly mug
and demand subservience at
the most inopportune of times.
The air smells sluttish, here:
your bedroom eyes glisten
like the half-life of recidivist
stars. I forgot to affix the
deadbolt, therefore we are
in danger. I'm done with
players, those only in it
for the food. My happy
meal is immaterial,
yet awaits, at the gate
where one billion people
have been served.
If I squint, I can see
the horizontal dimension,
a flatlined pulse.
Are you my people?
You call this a sunset?
Do not go anywhere.
I can make my body
into a starfish for you.

Theory of Everything

To be alive is to be present
at the quick takeover
of body, by mind.
To be dead is not to see
the white flannel curtain
that is the world before the window;
it's not to see the molecules of starch
on the freshly made bed,
or the quivering boy
wondering whether the world
will soon end, and how.
He extricates himself
from his environment.
He studies history, from
King David to Saint Paul.
He begins to levitate,
the way a painting begs
to emerge from two dimensions,
bruised skin and dappled fruit,
to announce its theme: the all.

Threnody

Who cares if beauty is hopeless? Hope is
what a sturdy uterus was built for: sad sack,
floating jellyfish without a means to repel.
People in exile write so many letters.
Voices crying out in the wilderness,
from the dark dungeon of penal servitude.
I define paradise as a place where there
are many places to cry other than dirty bathroom
stalls, my usual go-to. I define holy matrimony
as an exaltation of form, and doves. Good God,
our dying changed everything. Now insolence
rules the day, bookended by the workaday slog,
and desire is a tamed pit bull, lunging at its leash.
What is love? Baby, don't hurt me.
What is hate? Cocktail of Molotov.
We are an epistle that cannot be read
aloud, as it would bring scandal to our
tribe. Out of dark waters, the end.
Let's break bread together, then.
Let's combat, then dissolve.

Zeitgeist

Death is an allergen, a foment,
a farce. Death is a handler
of wild turkeys and other animals
with grotesque physiognomy,
like baboons. Death hates it
when the mariachi band comes
to town—death is the wet fish
that stands on the sidelines,
arms crossed, while even
the village fool is dancing.
Vanilla custard. Hot dogs.
These are among death's
favorite foods, because
contrary to popular opinion,
death eats, though not much,
and not with any pleasure.
Death is not to be confused
with swooning or injury,
even though both brush
his sleeve. Can't you
just imagine it: death
sipping a daiquiri
underneath a beach
umbrella, scowl
affixed, while the rest
of the world frolics
and bathes? Death
is the patternless pattern,
the soundless howl,
the irritant that can't
be soothed, or healed.
You live many times,

but you only die once.
This is death's glory,
the spirit of the age.

The lines "I choose you, my escaped convict / running ragged in the midst" in the poem "Apocrypha" were borrowed from Eileen G'Sell.

The lines "Who said the novel is a vaudeville show, / the six o'clock news, the mumblings / of wild men saddled by demons?" in the poem "Clair de Lune" are borrowed from Ishmael Reed.

The lines "In calligraphy, if a stroke falters, / you must begin the word all over again" in the poem "Ex Oblivione" are borrowed from Gillian Sze.

The lines "I am writing your name as if I were a Trojan / who expected someone else to smooth the shore" in the poem "Helen Keller at the Rodeo" are borrowed from Barbara Guest.

The line "I am a little world made cunningly" in the poem "Muta Cupido" is borrowed from John Donne. The line "I am a parcel of vain strivings, tied" in the same poem is borrowed from Henry David Thoreau.